*For my mother, who introduced me to the joy of exploring
the natural world. Her spirit lives in our hearts.   —D. S. M.*

For Char . . . my life of seventeen years.   —J. V. Z.

Disappearing Lake

Nature's Magic in Denali National Park

Debbie S. Miller ~ **Illustrations by Jon Van Zyle**

WALKER AND COMPANY

NEW YORK

In a wooded valley, the snow begins to melt.
Sparkling beads of water trickle together, growing into rivulets,
brooks, and streams. They speak to you in the language of water.
A snowy meadow laced with the tracks of moose and caribou,
wolf and bear, fox and raven, is changing.

Paths of water drain into the meadow from all directions.
Inch by inch, foot by foot, snow water floods the meadow.
The lake rises higher and higher, reaching up the surrounding
slopes. The trunks of cottonwoods wade in the growing lake.

Spring birds arrive from all corners of the earth. A bald eagle rests on the crown of a spruce tree. The eagle's sharp eyes scan the lake, searching for signs of fish. Insects that burrowed beneath leaves and grasses to survive the long winter awaken. Fairy shrimp hatch from tiny eggs and paddle through the water. Shorebirds land near the fringe of the lake and probe for a meal.

A robin gathers muddy twigs and grasses to build a nest in a nearby spruce. Whistling wings circle the lake. Webbed feet skim across the glassy water. Goldeneye ducks skitter after one another as the mating season begins.

On a warm day a cow moose and her new calf take a cool drink.
They browse on some willow buds near the shore of the lake.

In the evening, wolves prowl through the forest. A spring breeze carries the scent of moose, and the wolves quietly stalk their prey. They reach the edge of the lake. The lead wolf stands motionless. His glaring eyes meet the bold stare of the cow moose. She lays her ears back, ready to fight and protect the calf. After a short time, the wolves leave the lake to search for easier prey.

At dawn a wandering beaver looks for a new home.
He discovers the lake.
RASP, GRATE, SCRAPE.
The beaver gnaws down three cottonwoods,
the beginning of a new dam.

The days grow warmer. Butterflies bask in the sunshine, spreading their wings. Creeks dry up and no longer feed the lake. Inch by inch, foot by foot, the lake is disappearing.

The ducks move on to a bigger lake with more plants and fairy shrimp
to eat. The young beaver searches for a new home with more water.
A snowshoe hare nibbles on the cottonwoods that the beaver left behind.

The lake shrinks to the size of a big puddle, then disappears.
But the lake has left a gift. A group of caribou browse on
green plants that sprout from the soggy floor of the old lake.

Inch by inch, foot by foot, the grasses grow. The lake turns into a meadow. Creeks that bubbled and sang their way to the lake are now bright green paths specked with flowers and wild chives. A white-crowned sparrow visits the meadow, singing its joyful song.

The cow moose and calf return to the meadow and bed down in the soft grasses. Voles and shrews tunnel their way beneath tussock mounds. One vole gnaws on an old caribou bone that once lay on the bottom of the lake.

Summer wanes and the cottonwoods flutter their gold in the wind.
The robins and sparrows, eagles and shorebirds, ducks and swans,
cast off the chill of autumn and fly south.

The first snowflakes hush the meadow. Inch by inch, foot by foot,
the meadow disappears beneath the white of winter.
Tracks once again lace the snow beneath the dancing northern lights.

Field Notes

Bald Eagle: More bald eagles nest in Alaska than anywhere else in North America. Most bald eagles are found along the coast of Southeast Alaska, where they build huge stick nests on the tops of trees in old-growth forests. This large bird has a six- to eight-foot wingspan and feeds largely on fish.

Beaver: Beavers are found along rivers, ponds, and lakes of Alaska, where there is a good supply of trees for food and dam construction. The beaver is North America's largest member of the rodent family. Its sharp incisor teeth grow continuously for the beaver's whole life. The beaver that cut down the trees at Disappearing Lake was probably young and unaware that the temporary lake would soon dry up.

Butterflies: The green comma and mourning cloak are pictured in this story. The mourning cloak, with its unique yellow-fringed wings, hibernates beneath the snow in its adult phase. It is often the first butterfly Alaskans see in the spring when the snow begins to melt. Before flowers bloom, mourning cloaks often feed on the tree sap that drips from twigs that moose have browsed. The green comma also hibernates through the winter. Its name refers to the small white commas that appear on the green-specked underside of its wings.

Caribou: More caribou than people live in Alaska. About one million caribou in more than 30 distinct herds roam across the state. Caribou are the only members of the deer family in which both the male and the female grow antlers. New antlers are grown each summer and are covered with velvet. These regal deer graze primarily on lichens in the winter and on a variety of plants in the summer.

Ducks: Many species of ducks migrate to Alaska to breed. The common and Barrow's goldeneye ducks have wings that whistle when they fly. Like other ducks, goldeneyes nest in the area where the female duck was born. They build their nests in tree cavities. These diving ducks feed on plants, small fish, fairy shrimp, and other invertebrates.

Fairy Shrimp: These small freshwater crustaceans are an important food source for ducks and shorebirds. The fairy shrimp of Disappearing Lake have a short life cycle that lasts only a few weeks. Their eggs lie frozen beneath the snow most of the year.

Hares: There are two species of hares in Alaska. The snowshoe hare is commonly seen in the northern forest, and the larger tundra hare is found on Alaska's west and northwest coasts. These well-camouflaged animals are brown in the summer and white in the winter. Their large, furry hind feet act as snowshoes when they travel through deep snow.

Insects: Insects are an important food source for many migratory shorebirds, waterfowl, and songbirds. Disappearing Lake provides a home for many different species of insects, such as mosquitoes, diving beetles, caddisflies, and water striders.

Moose: The moose is the largest member of the deer family. Bull moose (males) stand about six feet tall at the shoulder and can weigh as much as 1,600 pounds. Moose calves are born in mid-May to early June and weigh about 30 pounds. A calf lives with its mother for about one year. Moose can be found throughout most of Alaska where there is a good food suppy of willows and birch shrubs.

Northern Lights: The shimmering curtains of northern lights, or the aurora borealis, can be seen on many nights in Alaska. The northern lights are caused by tiny particles that shoot through space from the sun. Known as the solar wind, these particles race toward Earth and mix with our planet's atmosphere near the magnetic poles. This creates halos of magical light that form above the North and South poles.

Rivulet: A narrow channel of water that flows into a brook or stream.

Robin: This common bird can be found year-round in most of the United States. Some robins migrate to Alaska to nest, even as far north as the Brooks Range. After the long winter, their melodious song is welcomed by Alaskans because it signals the return of summer.

Shorebirds: Shorebirds have long legs and pointed wings, and many species have beaks designed for probing in the sand, mud, or marsh for insects and other invertebrates. The shorebirds pictured in this book are lesser yellowlegs, a common visitor that has a loud, yodeling call. These strong fliers migrate to Alaska from as far south as Argentina.

Tussocks: Tussocks are cotton grass mounds that can be found across much of Alaska's tundra environment. These one- to two-foot-high bumps are designed to absorb heat from the sun. This enables the cotton grass and other plants growing on the tussock to bud sooner. Tussocks provide a good food source for herbivores, and shelter for voles and nesting birds.

Voles and Shrews: Several species of these mouselike mammals are found throughout Alaska. They provide an important food source for animals such as owls, foxes, weasels, and wolves. Voles sometimes gnaw on bones and antlers, good sources of calcium.

White-crowned Sparrow: This striking songbird nests in many areas of Alaska. Like other sparrows, this bird is largely a seed eater and lives in places with low shrubs near open, grassy feeding areas. Its whistling song is often heard around Disappearing Lake in the spring. These birds winter in the southern portion of the United States and in Mexico.

Wolf: Gray wolves are found in many areas in Alaska. They are highly social animals and cooperate together when hunting. These predators feed on moose, caribou, Dall sheep, small mammals, and fish. While wolves are considered endangered in many parts of the world, healthy populations exist in many areas across Alaska and Canada. An average wolf pack consists of six to twelve animals, with a territory that averages 600 square miles.